LEARN ABOUT
CAMERAS

CHRIS OXLADE

LORENZ BOOKS
LONDON • NEW YORK • SYDNEY • BATH

This edition published in the UK in 1997 by Lorenz Books

Lorenz Books is an imprint of
Anness Publishing Limited
Hermes House
88-89 Blackfriars Road
London SE1 8HA

This edition published in Canada by Lorenz Books, distributed by
Raincoast Books Distribution Limited, Vancouver

ISBN 1 85967 312 0

Publisher: Joanna Lorenz
Managing Editor, Children's Books: Sue Grabham
Editor: Ann Kay
Consultant: Peter Mellett
Photographer: John Freeman
Stylist: Marion Elliot
Designer: Caroline Reeves
Picture Researcher: Marion Elliot
Illustrators: Richard Hawke, Caroline Reeves

Printed and bound in China

1 3 5 7 9 10 8 6 4 2

The Publishers would like to thank the following pupils from Hampden
Gurney School: Gary Cooper, Diane Cuffe, Sheree Cunningham-Kelly,
Louisa El-Jonsafi, Sarah Ann Kenna, Lee Knight, Shadae Lawrence,
Robert Nunez, Kim Peterson, Paul Snow, Kisanet Tesfay. They would
also like to thank Keith Johnson and Pelling Ltd for the loan of props,
and Nikon UK Ltd and Intel Corporation UK for the loan of pictures.

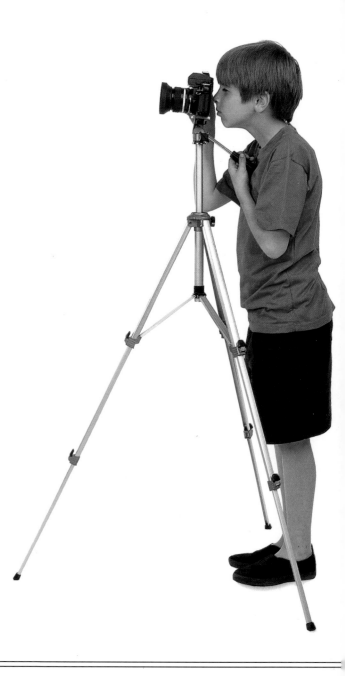

CAMERAS

CONTENTS

YOU AND YOUR CAMERA

WHAT is the one vital piece of equipment you must not forget if you are off on holiday? Your camera! To most people, a camera is simply a device for taking snapshots of their favourite places or people. But cameras are also sophisticated machines that make use of the latest breakthroughs in science and technology. A camera is designed to do a specific job – to make a copy of a scene on film by collecting light from that scene and turning it into a picture. It works in a very similar way to your eyes, but it makes a record of the scene instead of simply seeing it.

Open and shut
Using a camera is like looking through a special window. Open and close your eyes very quickly. This is how a camera records light from a scene.

With your camera, you can record all kinds of events, such as parties and holidays. A simple point-and-shoot compact camera is all you need.

Early cameras
The first practical cameras with film were developed in the 1830s. Today, cameras do the same job, but they are much easier to use. In the early days, it could take as long as half an hour to take a photo and the photographer had to stand under a large hood.

Producing prints

A camera is no use without a film inside to record the images the camera makes. If you want prints, then the film is developed, or processed, so that negatives are produced. Prints are then made from the negatives. Which of the negatives on this strip produced the print next to it?

Negative   *Print*

Getting it right

If a professional photographer is shooting a sports or news event, they must get it right. Their pictures appear in magazines and newspapers and help us to understand the story.

Professionals at work

Professional photographers usually need to use very sophisticated equipment to get the best result. They will probably carry two or three cameras, a selection of different lenses and dozens of rolls of film.

WHAT IS A CAMERA?

Aᴸᴸ cameras, from disposable to professional models, have the same basic parts. The camera body is really just a light-proof box. This keeps the light-sensitive film in complete darkness. The film is held flat in the back of the body. At the front of the body is the lens, which collects light from the scene and shines it onto the film. Between the lens and the film is a shutter. When you take a photograph, the shutter opens to let light hit the film.

Most cameras also have extra parts. These help you to take better photographs, or they may enable the camera to take photographs automatically, without the controls needing to be altered.

Disposable cameras come with the film already inside. You take the whole camera to the film processor when the film is finished.

Shutter release button

Viewfinder

Flash unit, to light up dark scenes

Compact camera

A compact camera is a small camera that will fit in your pocket. To take a photograph, all you have to do is aim at the scene and press the shutter release button. Simple compacts are also called point-and-shoot cameras.

Lens protected by plastic flap when camera not in use

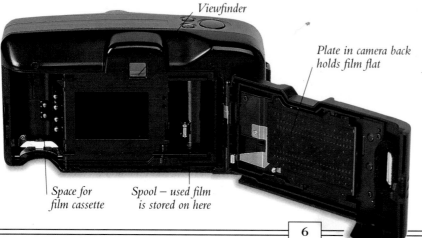

Viewfinder

Plate in camera back holds film flat

Space for film cassette

Spool – used film is stored on here

Inside the camera

You open the back of the camera to load and unload the film. There is space for the film cassette and a spool where the used film is stored. The film is advanced, or wound on, either by an electric motor or by hand.

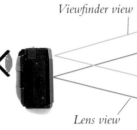

Viewfinder view

Lens view

You look through a viewfinder to see what will be in your photo. The guidelines you see in many viewfinders (seen in red here) show what area will be included. Here, the boy's hat will be chopped off.

Close-up care

The view that you see in the viewfinder of a compact camera is not quite the same as the view that the lens sees. This is because the viewfinder is higher up than the lens. Remember to leave some space around close-up objects in the viewfinder.

Instant photos

With most cameras, you have to send your films away to be turned into photographs. This Polaroid camera uses special film and produces prints almost instantly.

SLR camera

Single-lens reflex camera

This type of camera is called a single-lens reflex camera (SLR). When you look into the viewfinder, you actually look through the lens itself. This means you see exactly what the lens sees. You can take the lens off an SLR camera and replace it with another.

HOW A LENS WORKS

Making your own simple viewer will show you just how a camera lens collects light from a scene and makes a small copy of it on the film. The copy is called an image. Just like a real camera, the viewer has a light-proof box. At the front of the box is a pin-hole, which works like a tiny lens. The screen at the back of the box is where the film would be in a real camera. This sort of viewer is sometimes called a camera obscura. In the past, artists used the camera obscura to make images of scenes that they could copy in their drawings and paintings.

You will need: ruler, scissors, small cardboard box, card, sharp pencil, sticky tape, tracing paper.

Light rays
Light travels in straight rays. You can see this when you shine a torch. When you look at a scene, your eyes collect rays coming from every part of it. This is just what a camera does.

Make your own viewer

1 Using scissors, cut a small hole, about 2 cm by 2 cm, in one end of the cardboard box.

2 Now cut a much larger square hole in the other end of your cardboard box.

3 Cut a square of card 4 cm by 4 cm. Pierce a tiny hole in the centre with a sharp pencil.

Making an image with light

When you use your viewer, the pin-hole lets in just a few light rays from each part of the scene. The rays keep going in straight lines and hit the tracing paper screen, making an image of the scene.

If you look at a person through your viewer, light rays from their head hit the bottom of the viewer's screen. Rays from their feet hit the top of the screen. So the screen image is upside down. Left and right are swapped, too.

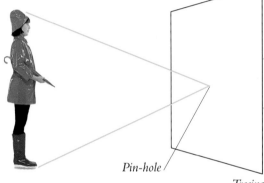

Pin-hole

Tracing paper screen

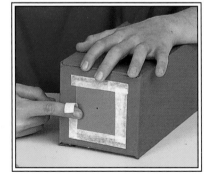

4 Put the card with its pin-hole over the box's smaller hole and tape it into place.

5 Cut a square of tracing paper slightly bigger than the larger hole and stick it over that hole.

6 Now look out of a window, through the tracing paper screen. Try tracing the scene onto the paper.

REFRACTION AND REFLECTION

A LIGHT ray keeps going in a straight line until it hits something. Then it usually changes direction, by bending or bouncing. When light rays bend, it is called refraction. For example, objects often look distorted if seen through certain types of glass, or through water. This is because the rays have been bent by the glass or the water. Reflection is the word used to describe rays that bounce off objects with shiny surfaces, such as mirrors. How does all of this apply to cameras? Camera lenses are made of specially shaped pieces of glass. They refract light rays in an organized way, turning them into a clear image on the film and also producing the picture in your viewfinder. Some cameras also have carefully angled mirrors to bounce rays off in a specific direction.

Light rays from the part of the straw that is under water bend as they pass through the surface. This makes the straw look bent.

Magnifying lens
A magnifying glass lens has a convex shape. This means that its faces curve outwards. It is this shape that makes rays passing through the lens converge.

Converging light rays
The lens of a magnifying glass makes light rays from objects converge, or bend inwards, towards each other. So, when they enter the eye, they seem to have come from a bigger object.

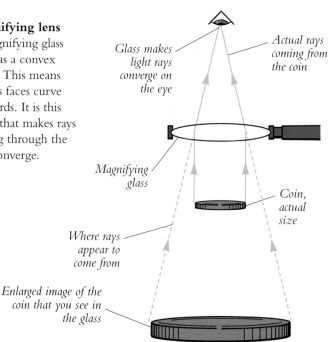

Glass makes light rays converge on the eye

Actual rays coming from the coin

Magnifying glass

Coin, actual size

Where rays appear to come from

Enlarged image of the coin that you see in the glass

Camera lenses

A magnifying glass is a single converging lens, but some camera lenses consist of several lenses. Each one is called an element and the light passes through all of them. Multiple-element lenses like the ones seen here help to prevent your images from having coloured edges. This is a particularly common problem with single-element lenses.

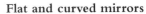

Flat and curved mirrors

Some cameras have one or more mirrors instead of a lens. All the rays that hit a mirror are reflected. A flat mirror *(left)* reflects all rays in the same way, so your image looks unchanged (although left and right seem reversed).

A convex mirror reflects and bends light *(right)*. It works like a mirror and a lens together to distort the image.

Film

Light rays

Lens

How a camera makes images

All camera lenses are converging lenses. They bend light rays from the scene inwards, towards each other. The light rays from any given part of your subject are bent so that they meet again on the other side of the lens. In a camera, they meet on the film.

EXPERIMENT WITH LIGHT

THE best way to see refraction and reflection at work is to create some light beams and then send them through lenses and bounce them off mirrors. You can make narrow light beams by shining a torch through slots in a sheet of card. Try these experiments and then see what ideas of your own you have. Carry out the experiments in a room with the lights off and the blinds down or curtains drawn. Pale-coloured card will work most effectively.

M A T E R I A L S

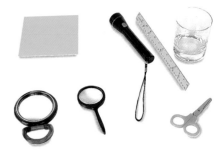

You will need: ruler, card, scissors, torch, glass of water, magnifying glass, mirror.

Having fun with beams

1 Cut slots 2 mm wide and 5 cm long in two pieces of card. Shine a torch through both to make a beam of light. These pictures are light so that you can see what is happening, but you will get the best effects in the dark.

2 Now put a glass of water in the path of the beam. Move the glass from side to side to see how the beam is refracted more or less.

3 Replace the second piece of card with one with three slots in it. Put a magnifying glass in the path of the three beams to make them converge.

Clear images

See how an SLR gives crisp images. Hold a glass of water up so that you can see the underneath surface of the water clearly. Now poke your finger into the water from above. You should see a clear, single reflection of your finger in the surface. This is because the surface acts like a mirror *(now see box below)*.

MIRRORS AND PRISMS

Stopping reflections

If you look very carefully at a reflection in a normal mirror, you can see a ghostly second image. The water mirror on this page does not make a ghost image. To stop you from getting ghost images, the SLR has a glass block called a pentaprism, which treats reflections in the same way as the water.

The same view

The pentaprism in an SLR camera also makes sure that the image you see in the viewfinder is the same as the image you see on your final photo.

4 Now try each of these, and put a mirror in the way of the different beams. Can you see how the pattern of rays stays the same?

GETTING INTO FOCUS

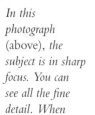

Before taking a photograph, you need to make sure that your subject is in focus. When it is, all the rays of light that leave a point on the subject are bent by the lens so that they hit the same place on the film. This makes a clear, sharp image of the subject. Parts of the scene in front or behind the subject will not be in sharp focus. You have to choose the part of the scene that you want to be in focus. On some cameras, you have to do the focusing yourself, but autofocus cameras do it automatically.

In this photograph (above), *the subject is in sharp focus. You can see all the fine detail. When the same shot is out of focus* (right), *it makes the subject look blurred.*

Getting closer
Use a magnifying glass and lamp to make an image of an object on a sheet of paper. Move the magnifying glass closer to and farther from the paper, to bring different parts of the scene into focus.

Focal plane

The focal plane
When the image of a subject is in focus, the light rays meet on a flat area called the focal plane. The camera's film is held flat in the focal plane. You can see the focal plane if you open the back of your camera.

Focusing SLRs
With an SLR camera, you see exactly what the image looks like through the viewfinder. On a manual-focus SLR, you turn a ring on the lens to get your subject in focus.

Viewfinder

Pentaprism

Lens

Light ray

Mirror

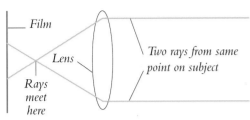

Film

Lens

Two rays from same point on subject

Rays meet here

The lens is too far from the film. Rays from the subject meet in front of the film, so it is out of focus.

In and out of focus

A camera focuses on a subject by moving the lens backwards and forwards so it gets closer to, or farther from, the film. This brings parts of the scene that are at different distances from the camera into focus.

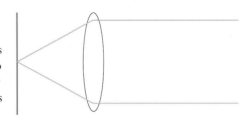

To focus, the lens is moved backwards, towards the film. The rays meet on the film.

Autofocus

With the type of autofocus system shown here, the camera emits a wide beam of invisible infra-red light. It works out how long the infra-red light takes to bounce back, and so knows how far away the subject is. A small electric motor then moves the lens.

Orange lines = beam travelling out to subject from camera
Red lines = beam bouncing back to camera from subject

Sends out beam

Top view of camera

Detector

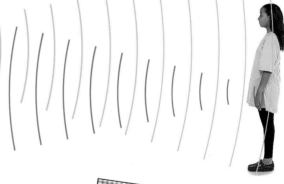

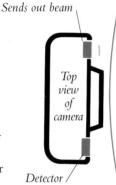

Autofocus errors

Most autofocus cameras focus on objects that are in the centre of the scene in the viewfinder. If your subject is off to one side, the camera focuses on the background, and your subject will be blurred *(left)*. If you have a focus lock, you can beat this by aiming at the subject first, and then using your focus lock before recomposing the shot and shooting *(right)*.

USING FILM

THE camera's job is to create a focused image of a scene, but this would be no use without a way of recording the image. This is the job of the film. Film contains chemicals that are affected by light. The more light that hits them, the more they are changed. So when an image hits the film, the chemicals record the patterns of light, dark and colour. You cannot look at film straight away. It must be developed with chemicals before the image shows up. Until then, it must be kept in the dark, or the whole film will react to light and be ruined.

Always load and unload a film in dim light or in shadow, to prevent light from leaking into the film canister.

Types of film

There are several different types of film. The most common one is the film you use when you want to end up with colour prints. This is called colour negative film. Other common types are colour reversal, or slide, film, and black and white negative film.

Exposing a film

Black and white film contains millions of microscopic light-sensitive crystals. In turn, these crystals contain silver. When a photograph is taken, some of the crystals that are exposed to light begin to break down, leaving metal silver. Where more light falls, more crystals begin to change.

Film

The film is exposed by the camera when you take your photo, of a bird on a light background (left).

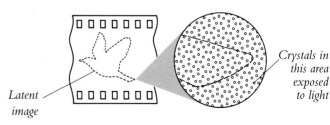

Latent image

Crystals in this area exposed to light

Crystals in the light area of the image change (above). Crystals in the dark area do not. The image has been recorded chemically. Nothing shows up on the film, and the image is called the latent image.

Processing film

Amateur photographers develop black and white films at home, in a small developing tank. In the dark, the film is wound carefully onto a plastic spiral. The spiral is then placed in the tank and the lid is put on. A chemical called developer is poured into the tank, left for a few minutes and poured away. Then chemical fixer is poured in. Finally, the film is washed.

Film drying

After washing, films are carefully dried. They are usually hung up to dry in a dust-free area, sometimes in a special drying cabinet. Once the films are dry, the photographer can examine them and choose the ones to print.

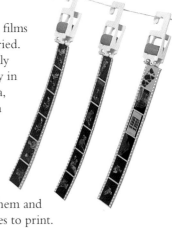

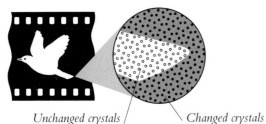

Black background with white bird

Unchanged crystals / Changed crystals

During developing (above), all the crystals that had begun to break down change completely to silver. They look black. The unchanged crystals stay as they are.

Black background with clear bird

No crystals / Changed crystals

Fixing (above) gets rid of all the unchanged crystals, leaving clear film. The result is a negative, where dark areas on the original subject are light, and light areas are dark.

Colour negative film looks strange because the colours are unnatural. The true colours are revealed when prints are made.

When slide film is developed, the actual colours of the scene are reproduced.

THE RIGHT FILM

All the details of a film (format, speed and length) are written on the film carton and the film cassette.

THE three basic types of film are colour negative film, colour slide film and black and white film. Films come in different sizes (called formats), and most cameras take 35-mm roll film. Films also come in different lengths. The lengths are measured by the number of exposures, or photographs, that will fit on the film. The usual lengths are 24 and 36 exposures. Another thing to decide is which speed of film you want to use. Fast films react to light more quickly than slow films. Film speed is called the ISO rating. The most common speeds are ISO 100 and ISO 200, which are medium-speed films.

Automatic coding
On one side of a film cassette is a pattern of black and silver squares. This is called a DX code and it indicates the film's ISO rating and length. Modern cameras have special sensors that can read the code. On older cameras, you have to set the ISO rating on a dial.

Which film speed?
The difference between films of different speeds is the size of their crystals (or grains). Fast films (ISO 400 and above) are perfect for shooting in dim light and for action shots. They have larger grains than slow films because larger grains can react to much less light than small ones. These large grains often show up in the final picture *(above right)*. Slow films (ISO 50 and below) are perfect for fine, crisp detail *(above left)*.

120 film

35-mm film

APS film

Disk camera film

110 film

Polaroid film

Film and photo formats

Format is the size of the film and the size and shape of each image recorded on the film. Large-format films give much more detail. Smaller formats are more convenient. Some cameras can take photographs of different formats on the same film.

Indoor films

Most colour films are designed for use in daylight. If you use them indoors, with light from light bulbs, the photos come out yellowy. You can buy special indoor film called tungsten film, which gives the right colours.

Winding on

Roll films have a row of small sprocket holes along each side. These fit over sprockets inside the camera, which turn to wind on the film after a photo has been taken. This brings a fresh part of unexposed film into place behind the lens.

Film with holes along edge

Sprockets

Used film stored on spool

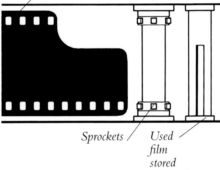

Polaroid film

The film used in Polaroid cameras is very different from other films. As well as the chemicals to record the image, it has developing chemicals inside.
After a photograph is taken, the film is squeezed through a roller, which releases the developer.
This turns the film into a finished photograph.

FACT BOX

• Infra-red film is special film with chemicals that react to the invisible heat, rather than the visible light, from a scene.

• The largest negative that has ever been used measured 7 m by 25 cm. This massive negative was made for a huge panoramic picture of 3,500 people, which was photographed in the USA in 1992.

• 35-mm format film was originally developed for movie cameras.

RECORDING AN IMAGE

Y OU do not need a camera to see how film works. In fact, you do not need a film either! You can use black and white photographic paper instead. Photographic paper is the paper that prints are made on. It works in the same way as film. Here, you can see how to make a picture called a photogram. It is made by covering some parts of a sheet of photographic paper with objects and then shining light on the sheet. When the paper is developed, the areas that were hit by the light turn black.

MATERIALS

You will need: lamp, photographic paper, different-shaped objects such as keys, discs and scissors, rubber gloves, protective goggles, plastic tongs, plastic dishes, chemicals (see below).

Photographic chemicals

You will need two photographic chemicals – developer for paper (not film) and fixer. Buy them from a photographic supplier. Ask an adult to help you follow the instructions on the bottles to dilute the chemicals. Store the diluted chemicals in plastic bottles. Seal the bottles and label them clearly.

Make your own photogram

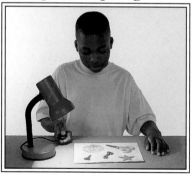

1 Turn off the light. Lay a sheet of photographic paper down, shiny side up. Put objects on it. Turn the light on again for a few seconds.

2 Pick up the paper with the tongs and put it into the dish of developer. Push it down so that the paper is under the liquid.

3 After a minute, use the tongs to move the paper into the fixer. Leave it right under the liquid for a minute, until an image appears.

Photographic paper

For black and white prints, you need a paper called monochrome paper. Buy the smallest size you can, and choose grade 2 if possible, with a gloss finish. The paper comes in a light-proof envelope. Only open the envelope in complete darkness.

This symbol, on photographic chemical bottles, means that they can be dangerous if not used with care. Always wear gloves and goggles.

The finished photogram should show the objects in white on a black background. Try experimenting with other ideas. How about cutting out letters and making your name?

4 Now you can turn the light back on. Lift the paper out and wash it with running water for a few minutes. Then lay the paper on a flat surface to dry.

THE CAMERA SHUTTER

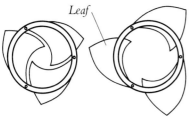

Leaf

A leaf shutter has thin metal plates called leaves. These overlap each other to close the shutter (left) and swivel back to open it (right).

ALL cameras have a shutter between the lens at the front and the film at the back. The shutter is rather like a door. It is closed most of the time, so that no light gets to the film. When you take a photo, the shutter opens briefly and then closes again, to let light from your subject reach the film. The time for which the shutter is open is called the shutter speed. Compact cameras have a leaf shutter close to the lens. SLR cameras, which have interchangeable lenses, have a focal-plane shutter, just in front of the film.

First curtain

Focal-plane shutter

This has two curtains. When the camera takes a photograph, the first curtain opens to let light hit the film. The second curtain follows closely behind, covering up the film again. The smaller the gap between the curtains, the faster the shutter speed.

Second curtain

Shutter speeds

Most photographs are taken with a shutter speed between 1/60 and 1/250 of a second. On some SLR cameras, you have to set the shutter speed by turning a dial *(below)*. Each setting gives a shutter speed about twice as fast as the one before.

Camera shake

When the shutter is open, even tiny camera movements make the image move across the film, causing a slightly blurred image. This is called camera shake. It can happen if the shutter speed is below about 1/60 of a second.

A tripod forms a steady base for a camera. It is very useful if you are taking photographs with slow shutter speeds because there is no chance of camera shake. Using a tripod will also help you to compose your pictures really well, because you do not have to worry about holding the camera.

There are several ways of keeping your camera steady as you take a photograph, even if you do not have a tripod. For example, stand with your legs slightly apart, or crouch down with one knee on the ground. Squeeze the shutter release button slowly. For extra steadiness, lean yourself against a wall, or try resting your camera on a wall.

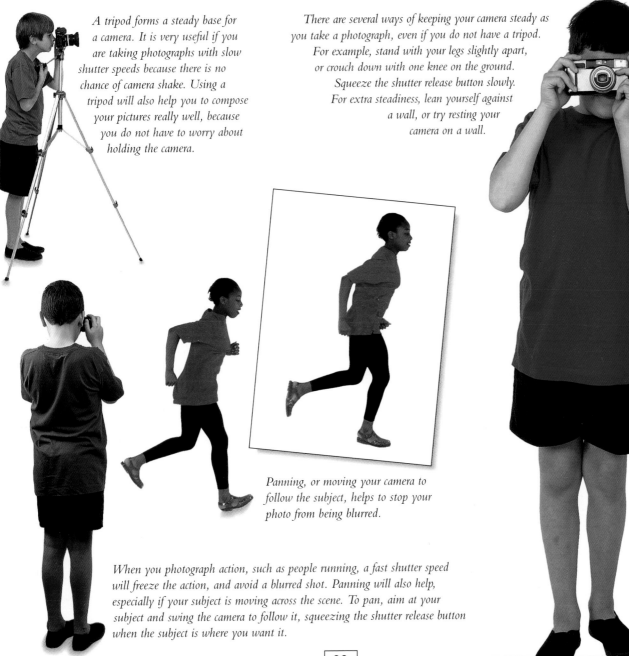

Panning, or moving your camera to follow the subject, helps to stop your photo from being blurred.

When you photograph action, such as people running, a fast shutter speed will freeze the action, and avoid a blurred shot. Panning will also help, especially if your subject is moving across the scene. To pan, aim at your subject and swing the camera to follow it, squeezing the shutter release button when the subject is where you want it.

THE APERTURE

The aperture ring on an SLR lens. Aperture size is measured in f-numbers (such as f/8).

MOST cameras have an aperture as well as a shutter. The aperture is behind the camera lens. It is basically a hole that can be made larger or smaller. When the aperture is small, some of the light rays that pass through the lens are cut off so that they do not reach the film. This does not cut off any of the image on the film, but it does reduce the amount of light that hits the film, making the image darker. Changing the size of the aperture also affects how much of the scene is in focus.

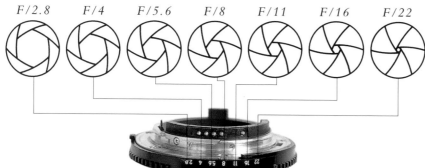

F/2.8   F/4   F/5.6   F/8   F/11   F/16   F/22

Aperture sizes
The mechanism that changes aperture size has interlocking metal leaves. These fold in to make the aperture smaller. The f-number is a fraction – f/4 means a quarter of the focal length of the lens, and so on. So an aperture of f/8 is half the width of one of f/4, and lets in one quarter the amount of light.

Changing depth of field
Depth of field is the distance between the nearest part of the scene that is in focus and the farthest part of the scene that is in focus. As f-numbers get bigger, the aperture gets smaller and the depth of field increases. Shooting on a sunny day will let you use a small aperture. This makes it easier to get a large depth of field.

F/2.8

F/8

F/16

In this photograph, the subject is in focus, and the background is totally out of focus. This is called a shallow depth of field because only objects a certain distance from the camera are in focus. Using shallow depth of field is ideal if you want to make parts of the scene that might confuse your picture disappear into a blur.

This photograph was taken with a much smaller aperture than the photograph on the left, making the depth of field far deeper. Almost everything in the scene is in focus. Greater depth of field is useful for photographs of scenery, especially if you have people in the foreground.

Try focusing your camera at a certain object and then changing the aperture. You will see how different areas of the picture come into focus.

FACT BOX

• A lens always has its maximum aperture written on it. For example, a lens described as 300 f/4 has a focal length of 300 mm and a maximum aperture of f/4.

• Large maximum apertures tend to be very expensive, because the lenses have to be much bigger! For example, an f/1.4 lens can cost several times as much as an f/4 lens.

• A pin-hole camera that is roughly the size of a shoe-box has an aperture of about f/500.

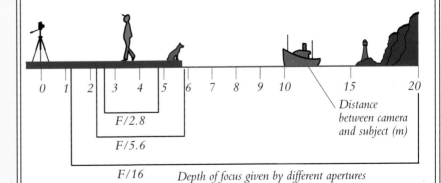

Distance between camera and subject (m)

Depth of focus given by different apertures

Lens focused at 3 m
Aperture at f/2.8
Depth of field = 1.5 m

Lens focused at 3 m
Aperture at f/5.6
Depth of field = 3.5 m

Lens focused at 3 m
Aperture at f/16
Depth of field = 20 m

THE RIGHT EXPOSURE

Here, too little light has reached the film, and the chemicals have not reacted enough. This is called under-exposure. The finished photo looks too dark.

EXPOSURE is the word for the amount of light that gets to the film in your camera when you take a photograph. Exposure depends on the shutter speed (slower shutter speeds allow more light through) and the aperture (larger apertures also allow more light through). You might see exposure stated as a combination of shutter speed and aperture, for example, 1/60 sec at f/16. All but the simplest cameras measure the amount of light coming from the scene and work out what exposure is needed for the speed of the film in the camera. They do this with an electronic light sensor called a metering system.

Here, too much light has got to the film, and the chemicals in the film have reacted too much. This is called over-exposure. The final photo is washed out.

When this photograph was taken, exactly the right amount of light reached the film, which has given the correct exposure. The finished picture is well-balanced – neither too light nor too dark.

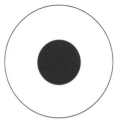
FACT BOX

• Some cameras can measure the changes in brightness across a scene and then take an average reading.

• There are certain advanced APS cameras that can remember the exposure settings for each picture.

• It is more important to get the exposure right if you are using slide film, rather than print film. This is partly because it is possible to correct mistakes when processing prints.

F/16 at 1/30 sec   *F/8 at 1/125 sec*   *F/4 at 1/500 sec*

Shutter speed and aperture

Try using different combinations of shutter speed and aperture, each of which lets in the same amount of light *(see above)*. For example, 1/125 seconds at f/8 is the same as 1/500 seconds at f/4 – the faster shutter speed is paired with a larger aperture. The combination you use depends on the type of photo you want. You might need a fast shutter speed for an action shot, or a small aperture for good depth of field in a landscape shot.

In this picture, the background is brighter than the main subject – the girl. This means that the camera measures only the light that is coming from the brighter area. As a result, the background is correctly exposed, but the girl herself is under-exposed and so looks too dark.

In this picture, the background was still by far the brightest part of the picture. The problem was solved, however, by using a much larger exposure and the lighting is just right. Bright lighting coming from the background is called back lighting.

LETTING IN THE LIGHT

Use a magnifying glass to investigate how changing a camera's aperture affects both the brightness of an image and the depth of field. To see an aperture at work, look at your own eyes. Like an aperture, your pupils automatically narrow in bright light to protect your retinas, and open wide to let you see in dim light. To see a shutter at work, open the back of your camera (when there is no film in it). Now look for a leaf shutter near the lens or a focal-plane shutter.

You will need: cardboard tube, thin card, magnifying glass, tracing paper, pencil, scissors, sticky tape, table lamp.

Use your eyes
Look closely at one of your eyes in a mirror. Close it and, after a few seconds, open it again quickly. You should see your pupil go from wide to narrow as your eye detects the bright light.

Apertures

1 Carefully attach the magnifying glass to one end of your cardboard tube with small pieces of sticky tape.

2 Roll a piece of thin card around the other end of the tube. Stick its edge down to make another tube that slides in and out.

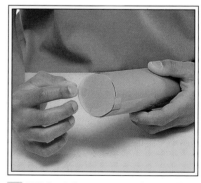

3 With sticky tape, attach a circle of tracing paper across the end of the sliding card tube. This will form your viewing screen.

See a shutter at work
To see just how a shutter works, open the back of your camera (when there is no film inside) and carefully place a small strip of tracing paper where your film usually goes. Now aim the camera at a subject, preferably one that is brightly lit, and press the shutter release button. You should see a brief flash of the image on your tracing paper.

4   With the screen nearest to you, aim your tube at a table lamp that is turned on. Can you see an image of the bulb on the screen?

5   Adjust the tubes until the image of the bulb is clear. Now adjust them again so that the image is slightly out of focus.

6   Cut a small hole (about 5 mm wide) in a piece of card, to make a small aperture. Look at the light bulb again and put the card in front of the lens. The smaller aperture will bring the light bulb into focus.

PRINTING

WHEN a film is developed, the images on the film are usually too small to look at. You can view slide films with a projector, which makes a large copy of the image on a screen. But before you can look at photographs taken with negative film, you have to make prints. The paper used for prints is light-sensitive, just like film. To make a print, the negative image is projected onto the paper. When the paper is developed, you get a negative of the negative (a positive), so that the scene appears as you saw it originally.

If you are using black and white film, remember that bright areas of the image change the chemicals in the film more than dark areas.

Negatives
When black and white film is processed, light areas of the scene appear dark and dark areas appear light. This is a negative.

Enlarging
This *(below)* is the first stage in making a print. An enlarger projects the negative onto paper placed below it. This must be done in the dark, so that no stray light spoils the paper. Lighter areas of the negative allow more light to get to the paper than darker areas.

Developing and fixing
The paper is processed in the dark, with chemicals *(above)*. Areas where light has hit the paper come out dark. So light areas of the negative come out dark, as in the original scene. These pictures look red because they have been taken in a photographer's dark room.

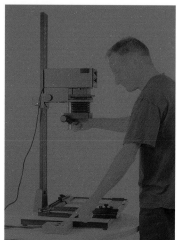

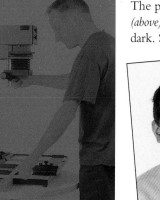

The final print
After processing, the final print must be dried to prevent it being damaged.

Colour photos

When you take a photo with colour negative film, the film records the patterns of colour in a scene. When the film is developed, the colours on the film look very strange, but the prints come out correctly. Colour film has three layers, one on top of the other, that can react to all of the different colours in the light spectrum.

Printing in colour

Colour prints are produced in the same way as black and white prints. The negative *(above)* is projected onto colour photographic paper. When the paper is developed, the colours are reversed once again, so that they come out looking natural.

FACT BOX

• The negative/positive method of photography was invented in 1839, by an Englishman called William Fox Talbot.

• High-contrast printing paper makes blacks look blacker and whites look whiter. Low-contrast paper creates less of a difference between the blacks and the whites.

• Professionals can make parts of a print look lighter or darker by using special techniques on the enlarger. For example, they can burn certain areas, which means making more light get to them.

Processing and printing

Most people have their films sent away to be processed and printed *(right)* by a special photographic laboratory. Some shops, however, have their own automatic processing and printing machines, often called mini-labs. These can produce prints on the spot in a very short space of time.

YOUR OWN CAMERA

Y OU can make your very own simple camera with just a few basic pieces of equipment. The following project combines all the main principles that lie behind photography. For simplicity, this camera uses photographic paper instead of film, and a pin-hole instead of a lens. When the 'film' (paper) is processed, you will have a negative. Then turn to pages 34 and 35 to find out how you can make a print from it. Find out about the equipment you need by looking at pages 20-21.

Make a pin-hole camera

Then turn to pages 34 and 35 to find out how you can make a print from it. Find out about the equipment you need by looking at pages 20-21.

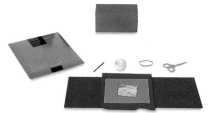

You will need: pin-hole box viewer, kitchen foil, scissors, sticky tape, pencil, black paper, thin card, thick cloth or plastic, photographic paper, elastic band.

1 Make the pin-hole viewer from the project on pages 8-9, but leave off the tracing-paper screen. Replace the card square with kitchen foil. Pierce a hole, about 2 mm across, in the centre of the foil with a pencil.

2 Cover as much of the inside of the box as you can with black paper, or colour the inside with a black felt pen.

3 Cut a square of card large enough to cover the kitchen foil. Tape just one edge to the box, so that it will act as a shutter.

4 Cut a square of card to fit right across the other end of the box. Tape it to one edge so that it closes over the hole like a door.

5 Find some light-proof cloth or plastic. Cut a piece large enough to fold over the end of the box.

6 In a completely dark room, put a piece of photographic paper under the flap at the end of the box. (*Note: these pictures are red because they were taken in a totally dark room.*)

7 Close the flap, wrap the cloth over it, and put an elastic band around the box to keep it secure.

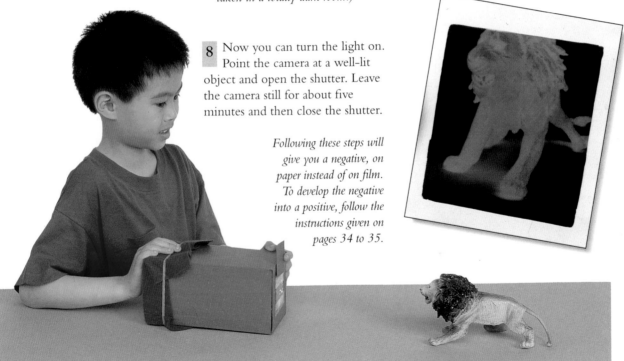

8 Now you can turn the light on. Point the camera at a well-lit object and open the shutter. Leave the camera still for about five minutes and then close the shutter.

Following these steps will give you a negative, on paper instead of on film. To develop the negative into a positive, follow the instructions given on pages 34 to 35.

PRINTING AND PROJECTING

I F you have just taken a photograph with your own pin-hole camera, you can find out how to turn it into a print below. There is also a simple projector for you to make. A projector lets you look at slide films – a type of film where the colours of the image on the processed film are the same as the colours in the original scene. You can think of projecting a photographic image as the reverse of taking a picture. First, light is shone right through the film. The light then goes through the lens of the projector and is focused on a screen, forming a large copy of your image.

A slide viewer is a special magnifying glass used for looking at slides. It is a convenient alternative to a projector.

M A T E R I A L S

You will need: photographic paper and chemicals, negative from pin-hole camera, torch or table lamp, safety goggles, rubber gloves, plastic dishes, plastic tongs or tweezers.

Quick and easy prints

1 In a totally dark room, lay a fresh sheet of photographic paper on a flat surface, shiny side up. Lay the negative from your pin-hole camera face-down on top.

2 Shine a torch or a table lamp onto the top of the two papers for a few seconds. Turn the torch off and remove your paper negative. Put on the goggles and gloves.

3 Develop, fix and wash the fresh paper. You should end up with a print of the original image *(right)*.

Do-it-yourself projector

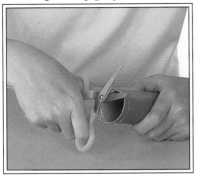

1 Cut two slots in the sides of the cardboard tube at one end, so that a strip of negatives will slide through. Only use old negatives that you do not want prints from any more.

2 Wrap card around the other end of the tube. Tape down the edge of a piece of card to make another tube that slides over the first.

3 Tape the magnifying glass to the end of the adjustable tube. Now tape a disc of tracing paper over the slotted end of the main tube.

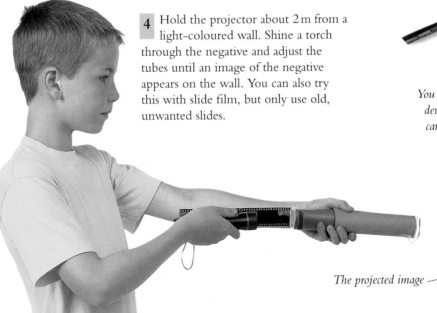

4 Hold the projector about 2 m from a light-coloured wall. Shine a torch through the negative and adjust the tubes until an image of the negative appears on the wall. You can also try this with slide film, but only use old, unwanted slides.

M A T E R I A L S

You will need: cardboard tube, scissors, developed colour negative film, thin card, sticky tape, magnifying glass, tracing paper.

The projected image

WIDE AND NARROW

What the lens sees
Put your hands either side of your face. Your view is similar to what a 50-mm lens can see.

Aᴸᴸ camera lenses have their own focal length, which is written somewhere on the lens. The focal length is the distance between the centre of the lens and the focal plane where it creates an image of a distant object. Lenses of different focal lengths produce images on the film that contain more or less of a scene. If you look in the viewfinder of a 35-mm camera with a 50-mm lens, you see about the same amount of the scene as you do with your eyes. Lenses with shorter focal lengths take in more of the scene, and longer lenses take in less.

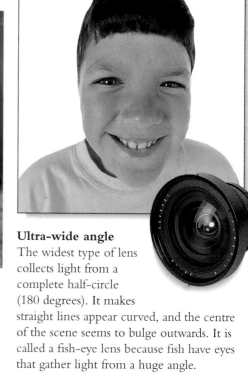

Ultra-wide angle
The widest type of lens collects light from a complete half-circle (180 degrees). It makes straight lines appear curved, and the centre of the scene seems to bulge outwards. It is called a fish-eye lens because fish have eyes that gather light from a huge angle.

Long-lens wobble
With telephoto lenses, which have very long focal lengths (300-mm or more), the tiniest bit of camera shake blurs the image. Professionals always use a tripod or monopod with these lenses, to keep the camera steady. This is also important because the amount of light that gets into the lens is quite small, and so slow shutter speeds are often needed.

Compacts

Some compact cameras have lenses that give wide and narrow views. The simplest ones usually have a 35-mm lens. This gives a slightly wider view *(left)* than you see with your own eyes.

Compact camera with variable lens

A wide-angle lens view

A telephoto lens view

Wide-angle lenses

Any camera lens that gives a wider view than we usually see with our eyes is called a wide-angle lens. Extremely wide-angle lenses (of 28-mm and less) allow you to get a huge amount of a scene into your photograph. A really wide-angle lens is perfect to use for panoramic photographs of scenery – such as cityscapes.

Telephoto lens

Any lens that gives you a magnified view of a scene is called a telephoto lens. A telephoto lens is a bit like a telescope, because it homes in on just one part of the scene. Telephoto lenses are often used to photograph portraits and distant wildlife, and for coming in close on the small details in a scene.

GETTING CLOSER

A compact camera with a built-in zoom lens. Pressing a button on the camera makes the zoom get longer or shorter.

To save carrying several different lenses with different focal lengths, many photographers have lenses that can change their focal length. These are called zoom lenses. They allow you to change how much of a scene will be in a shot without moving. The built-in lens on many compact cameras, and the lens that comes with most SLRs, is a zoom. A common zoom is 35-70, which means the lens can have focal lengths between 35 mm and 70 mm. It goes from wide angle to short telephoto (which brings objects closer). Macro, or close-up, lenses can focus on things very close to the lens. They are ideal for shots of flowers and insects.

SLR zooms

With an SLR and two interchangeable zoom lenses, such as 28-70 and 75-300, you can have a huge range of focal lengths. The focal length is changed by turning or sliding a wide ring on the lens. Because zoom lenses are so complicated, they can make straight lines in a scene look slightly bent.

A photograph taken at the 28-mm setting on a 28-200 zoom lens.

Super-zooms

A super-zoom lens has a very large range of focal lengths. For example, a 28-200 zoom goes from very wide angle to long telephoto.

Zooming in for detail with a 200-mm setting.

Close-up equipment
Special high-powered microscope cameras are used for some extreme close-ups, especially for scientific and nature subjects *(left and right)*.

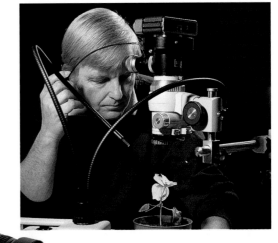

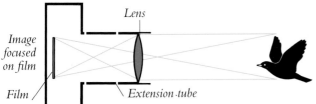

Extension tubes
An extension tube *(left)* fits between the camera body and the lens. It moves the lens farther from the film. This means that the lens can bend light rays into focus from objects that would usually be too close. A set of extension tubes has three tubes of different lengths for different magnifications.

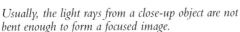

Image falls behind film

Lens

Film

Usually, the light rays from a close-up object are not bent enough to form a focused image.

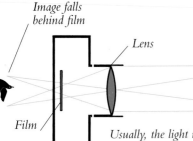

Image focused on film

Lens

Film

Extension tube

With an extension tube, the lens moves forwards, giving room for the rays to become focused.

FACT BOX
- A telephoto doubler fits between an SLR and its lens. It doubles the focal length of the lens.

- A 500-mm telephoto lens with a maximum aperture of f/8 weighs several kilograms.

- The longest lenses you can buy have a focal length of 1000 to 1200 mm.

- A standard 50-mm lens might be made up of 5 glass lenses. Most zoom lenses contain at least 12 lenses.

FOCAL LENGTHS

I F you have either an SLR camera or a compact camera with a zoom lens, then you will probably have taken photographs at different focal lengths. The simple experiments shown on these two pages will help to explain how different focal lengths make more or less of a scene appear on the film. In the mini experiment on the left, try to find as many convex lenses as you can to experiment with. You will find that weaker lenses, which have longer focal lengths, make larger images. This is the opposite to what happens if you use them as a magnifying glass.

Working with lenses
Standing by a window, use a magnifying glass to form an image of the window on a piece of paper. See what happens when you use different convex lenses.

M A T E R I A L S

You will need: cardboard tube, thin card, tracing paper, sharp pencil, sticky tape, scissors.

Zooming in and out

1 Cover one end of a cardboard tube with thin card. Pierce a small hole in the centre of the card with a sharp pencil.

2 Wrap a large square of card around the other end of the tube. Tape the edge down to form a sliding tube.

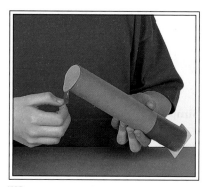

3 Cut out a circle of tracing paper that is big enough to stick over the end of your sliding tube. Tape it firmly in place.

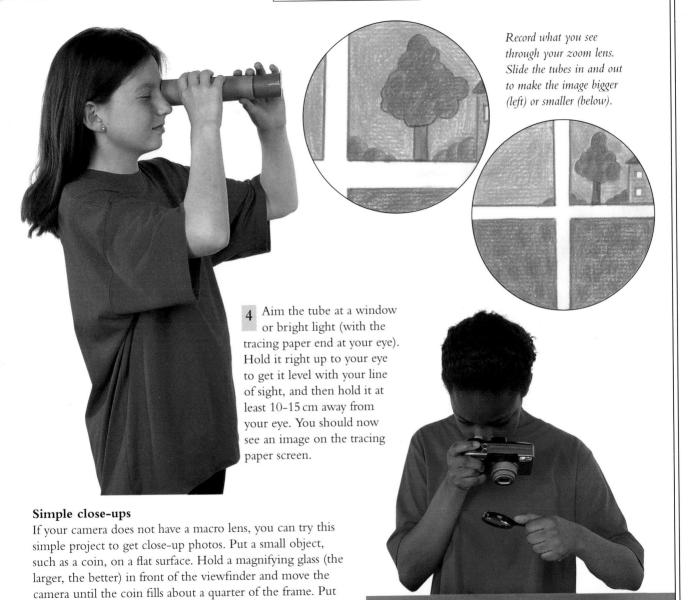

Record what you see through your zoom lens. Slide the tubes in and out to make the image bigger (left) or smaller (below).

4 Aim the tube at a window or bright light (with the tracing paper end at your eye). Hold it right up to your eye to get it level with your line of sight, and then hold it at least 10-15 cm away from your eye. You should now see an image on the tracing paper screen.

Simple close-ups

If your camera does not have a macro lens, you can try this simple project to get close-up photos. Put a small object, such as a coin, on a flat surface. Hold a magnifying glass (the larger, the better) in front of the viewfinder and move the camera until the coin fills about a quarter of the frame. Put the magnifying glass in front of the camera lens and take the photograph. Take a few more shots with the camera a bit nearer and then a bit farther away from the coin.

LIGHTING AND FLASH

LIGHTING is one of the most important parts of photography. The kind of light you take your picture in, how that light hits the subject, and where you take the picture from, all affect the result. Outdoors, most photos are taken with natural light. Artificial light is needed indoors, or outdoors when there is not enough natural light. Although photos can be taken in dim natural light, without additional artificial light, exposures usually have to be too long. Lighting can also create dramatic effects. Flash lighting makes a very bright light for a fraction of a second. Most small cameras have a small flash unit built in.

With front lighting, light is coming to the subject from the same direction as the camera. It lights the subject evenly, but gives a flat look because there are no strong shadows.

Back lighting means that the light is coming from behind the subject, so that the subject is between the light and the camera. This can often make your subject look very dark compared to the background.

If a picture is side-lit, then the light is coming across your subject. Side lighting will often give the best photographs, because it creates shadows that give more shape to the subject.

Lights and reflectors

Photographic studios *(left)* have lots of strong lights. They allow the photographer to create many different lighting effects, without worrying about natural light. Some lights make light over a wide area, others make narrow beams. Umbrellas and sheets of reflecting material help to direct the light, too.

Light in a flash

Light from a flash unit only lasts for a fraction of a second. It is carefully timed to flash when the camera's shutter is open. Many cameras have a built-in flash unit. A more powerful flash gun can be added to an SLR camera *(left)*. Most cameras tell you when you need to use the flash.

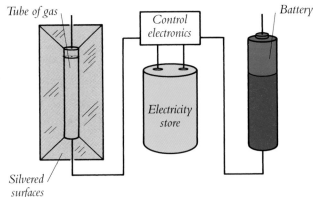

Tube of gas

Control electronics

Battery

Electricity store

Silvered surfaces

Inside a flash

Flash *(above)* is made by sending a very large electric current through a narrow tube of gas. This makes a lightning-like flash. The flash's batteries gradually build up a store of electric charge, which is released very quickly. It is like filling a jug from a dripping tap and then pouring all the water out at once.

These people are sitting at different distances from the flash. This means that some of them are overexposed, while others are underexposed.

Arrange people so that they are all about the same distance from the camera. This should ensure that everyone is properly exposed.

Bouncing and diffusing

Direct flash from the camera to the subject can cause harsh shadows and red-eye (where light bounces back from a person's eyes and makes them look red). Bounce flash means aiming the flash at the ceiling, so that the light spreads out. A diffuser is a sheet of material, like tissue paper, that softens the flash light.

WORKING WITH LIGHT

Red eye is caused by light from a flash unit near the camera lens bouncing off the retina (at the back of the eye) and back into the lens. With SLR cameras, the flash can be moved to one side to avoid red eye.

YOU can improve many of your photographs by thinking about the lighting before you shoot. For pictures of people, try some of the simple suggestions here to light up their faces in a new way. Outside, move around your subject to study how the light falls on it from different directions. Choose the best position before you take your photo. Ask people you are photographing to move so that the sunlight lights up their faces. If you cannot do this, some cameras have a back-light button that lengthens the exposure time for dark subjects. You could also add some flash to light up the darker areas. This is known as using fill-in flash.

MATERIALS

You will need: a camera, large sheets of white and coloured paper or card, kitchen foil, desk lamp, torch, coloured tissue paper.

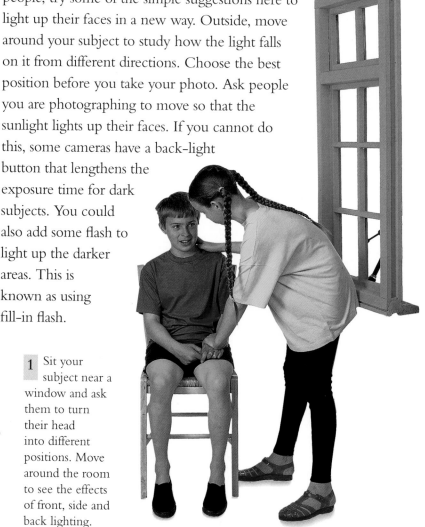

1 Sit your subject near a window and ask them to turn their head into different positions. Move around the room to see the effects of front, side and back lighting.

2 Hold a sheet of white paper or card near your subject to reflect some light from the window back onto their face. The reflected light fills in the shadows caused by the side lighting. Do the same with coloured paper. This will add colour to your subject's face.

3 Try the same with kitchen foil or a piece of shiny card. See how this gives a much brighter reflected light.

4 For pictures with some really spooky lighting effects, light your subject from below with an ordinary lamp or a torch. Do this in a darkened room. If you want to try out this kind of effect, you will probably need to get a friend to help.

5 To take this approach even further, experiment with putting your hand in front of the light. With this, and the previous step, turn off your camera's flash if you can, and hold the camera very still. If you have a tripod, use that.

6 For less harsh lighting, put a sheet of tissue paper in front of the lamp or torch. Try this with coloured tissue paper to see what effects you can achieve. You can also take flash photos with a small piece of tissue paper over the flash unit.

USING FILTERS

A PHOTOGRAPHIC filter changes the light as it enters the camera's lens. There are hundreds of different filters, and each one creates its own effect. The most common filter is called a skylight filter. It lets all visible light through the lens, but stops invisible ultra-violet light from getting in, as ultra-violet light can make photographs look unnaturally blue. Filters called graduate filters make some parts of the scene darker. They are often used to darken very bright skies. Coloured filters, such as red or yellow, can improve black-and-white photography. There are also all kinds of special-effect filters that you can buy, for adding different effects to your photographs.

It is usually only SLR cameras that use filters. Some filters are circular, and screw onto the end of the camera's lens. Others are designed to slot into a filter holder at the front of the lens.

Bright lights
You will not always want strong reflections and bright light in a picture *(below)*.

Polarizing filter
Here *(above)*, putting a special polarizing filter in front of the lens has made the reflections and strong light disappear. These filters cut out certain light rays from a scene, but let others through. They can also make the sky look more blue.

Creating a sunset

With a sunset filter, you can turn a daytime sky *(above left)* into a beautiful sunset *(above right)*. Half the filter is clear and the other half has a slight orange tint. With the tint positioned at the top of your shot, the sky appears orange.

Interesting shapes

A frame filter is a black mask with a shape cut in it. This makes the scene you are shooting come out in the same shape. The other parts of the scene will be black. Frame filters come in simple shapes, such as squares and ovals, and more complex shapes, such as keyholes.

Making your own

Make filters from transparent, coloured sweet wrappers. Put clean wrappers in front of the viewfinder to see what happens. Then attach them to the front of the lens with small pieces of tape and secure with an elastic band.

USEFUL TIPS

Hᴇʀᴇ are a few simple tips that should help you to improve your photographic technique and avoid some common mistakes. Good technique is made up of technical skill and an eye for an interesting subject. Remember that a complicated SLR camera does not necessarily take the best photographs, and that great shots are perfectly possible with a simple point-and-shoot camera. The first thing to decide is the type of film you want to use (colour print, colour slide or black and white). Always load and unload your film in dim lighting, and get it developed quickly once it has all been exposed.

Hold a camera steady with both hands. Be careful not to put your fingers over the lens, flash or autofocus sensor. Squeeze the shutter release button slowly.

Check the background
When you are taking portraits, or photographs of groups of people, always look in the background as well as at your subject. If necessary, recompose your photograph to avoid the sort of accident in this shot. Many cameras have a special portrait setting that gives a shallow depth of field, which automatically makes the background go out of focus.

Fill the frame
Do not be afraid to get close to your subject. For example, if you are taking a portrait, make sure the person's head and shoulders fill the frame *(left)*. But be careful not to get too close, because the camera may not be able to focus *(right)*. If you get too close with an autofocus camera, it will not let you take a picture.

Natural frames
Try adding some interest to photos by shooting through archways or doors to frame the subject. With photos of groups or scenery, you can include overhanging branches in the foreground.

The rule of thirds
Try using the rule of thirds – placing the subject a third of the way across or up or down the frame – to make the shot more interesting. With autofocus cameras, you often have to use your focus lock to point at the subject first and then recompose the picture before shooting.

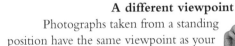

A different viewpoint
Photographs taken from a standing position have the same viewpoint as your eyes usually do. Changing the camera's viewpoint can give more interesting results. Try kneeling, or even lying down.

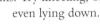

Bad weather photographs
You do not always need to wait for good weather before taking photos. In fact, overhead sunshine tends to give flat, dull pictures. Stormy clouds can be much more interesting than cloudless skies.

SPECIAL PHOTOGRAPHY

MOST cameras and lenses are designed for general photography. However, there are some types of camera that take photographs in unusual formats or in special conditions. For example, you can use special cameras to take really wide panoramic views, or to shoot scenes entirely under the water. There are also some unusual types of film. Some produce odd colours or shades in your photographs.

Another type of film records technical information about each of the shots.

Disposable underwater cameras can take photographs while completely under water. The camera's body is recycled after the film is processed.

Underwater SLRs

Divers take photographs under water with special SLR cameras that are waterproof even when they are many metres down. They can also withstand the high pressure of being deep under water.

If you want to photograph anything deep down under the water, you need to use extremely bright lights.

Panoramic photos

Panoramic cameras can take very wide photographs, which are good for shots of large groups of people or landscapes. Many compact cameras take pictures that are called panoramic, but they actually only appear to be so. They are no wider than a standard frame, just shorter.

Laser photographs

A hologram is a three dimensional (3-D) picture that looks 3-D no matter what angle you look at it from. The picture changes as you move your head from side to side. However, holograms are not taken with a camera. Another kind of equipment is used to record how laser light bounces off the subject from different directions.

Advanced systems

Many new compact cameras (and some SLRs) work according to the APS, or the Advanced Photographic System. They use a special type of film that records information about each shot.

FACT BOX

• Certain cameras are able to decide themselves whether a scene is a portrait, a landscape, or an action shot, and adjust the aperture and shutter to suit.

• APS film is similar to 35-mm film. It records information, such as the exposure settings and frame size, on a special magnetic layer and this is used during processing.

• You can also buy disposable panoramic cameras.

AMAZING EFFECTS

D ISCOVER how to take stereo photos and how to view them to get an amazing three-dimensional effect. It is easier than you might think, and you can do it with the most basic camera. Simply take two photos of the same scene from different places. The effect works because, like many animals, humans have binocular vision. This means that the two views from our different eyes overlap. In the overlapping area, our eyes see slightly different views, which makes things appear in three dimensions. After you have tried this experiment, you can find out how to build up a grand panoramic picture of a scene.

Place your stereo pairs of photographs side by side to view them.

The diagram on the right shows why stereo experiments work – because our two eyes see slightly different views.

Left eye sees this view

Top of head

Right eye sees this view

The actual 3-D box you are looking at

Make your model come alive

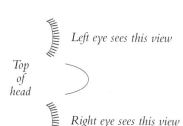

You will need: camera, model.

1 Choose a simple object such as this model of a dinosaur. Holding the camera very steady, take a picture. Try to include a bit of space around your subject.

2 Take a step about 20 cm to your left, and take another photo. Try taking more pairs of photographs, using different distances between the two photographs.

3 Put your pictures down side by side on a flat surface. Place your index finger between them. Look directly down onto the pictures and slowly raise your finger towards your nose, keeping it in focus. The two images should merge into one 3-D image. Try it with these two model dinosaur pictures.

Make a panorama

Choose a good general scene, with no close-up objects in it. Now, using a camera lens set at 35 or 50 mm, take a series of photographs that overlap slightly. When your prints are developed, lay them out to recreate all of your scene. When you are happy with the arrangement, tape them together carefully.

This completed panorama works well because it is a simple, open scene. If it had been filled with small objects, then the effect might not have been as good. If you want people in your scene, try to keep them away from areas that will overlap in the finished panorama.

MOVING PICTURES

A CINE camera is used to take moving pictures. It takes a whole series of photographs in quick succession (usually about 25 every second), on a very long roll of film. Any moving object appears in a slightly different position in each frame. When the photographs are displayed quickly, one after the other, the movement in the original scene appears to be recreated. The films are usually transparency, or positive rather than negative, films, and are put into a projector to be shown. Today, cine cameras are used mainly for professional movie-making. Home cine cameras used to be very popular, but today they have been replaced by video cameras.

Moving pictures rely on the fact that we have persistence of vision. This means our eyes remember a picture for a split second. To see how this works, look at a scene and close your eyes quickly.

Recording motion
The first movie cameras were made to record and study animal motion rather than for entertainment. This sequence was taken by British photographer Eadweard Muybridge (1830-1904).

Cine film
This is just like the rolls of film you put in a stills, or ordinary, camera. In fact, 35-mm film was originally made for cine cameras. The image in each frame of the film is slightly different to the one before.

Inside a cine camera

A cine camera has similar parts to a stills camera – a lens, shutter and aperture. It also has some extra parts for taking photos in quick succession. The film is wound on, ready for the next frame, while the shutter is closed *(right)*. The shutter speed is always the same and the exposure is controlled just by the aperture.

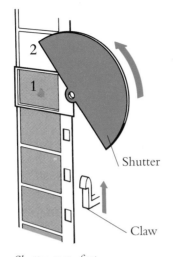

Shutter

Claw

Shutter open, first frame exposed

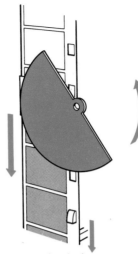

Shutter closed, claw pulls film down

Shutter open, second frame exposed

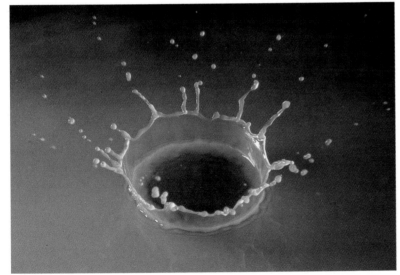

High-speed photos

This is a frame from a high-speed film. Some cine cameras can take hundreds, or even thousands, of photographs every second. When they are played back at normal speed, the action is slowed right down.

FACT BOX

• The world's fastest cine cameras are used by scientists. They can take 600 million frames every second.

• If you used a cine camera like this to film a bullet fired from a gun, the bullet would take 1000 frames to move just one millimetre.

• Like normal camera film, cine camera film comes in different formats. The most common format is 35-mm.

• In an IMAX cinema, the screen is as high as seven elephants on top of each other.

• On IMAX film, the frames are four times larger than 35-mm film.

ANIMATION

ANIMATION is making inanimate objects, or objects that cannot move by themselves, appear to move. Frames of the film are photographed one at a time with a special cine camera. Between each frame, the objects are moved slightly. When the finished film is viewed, the objects seem to move. Some animated objects are models, which are photographed to make animated movies. Others are drawings, which are photographed to make cartoons. Cartoon animation is often done by computer, so the photography stage is not needed.

Photo flick-book
The simplest way of making moving pictures is to put all the frames into a book and flick through the pages. In the 19th century, flick-books of photographs (called filoscopes) were popular toys. You can see some of the pages from an old filoscope above.

This picture shows a scene from one of the highly popular Wallace and Gromit *films, made by Aardman Animations Ltd. Model animation is a highly skilful and time-consuming job. The models must be moved very, very slightly between each frame.*

Background cels

Cartoon cels

Until the 1980s, cartoons were made by photographing drawings. The drawings were done on transparent plastic sheets called cels. Moving characters were drawn on one cel and the still background on another, to save drawing the background again and again for each frame *(right)*. Once the cels were completed, they were photographed with a cine camera. When these were shown in rapid succession, a moving film appeared.

Character cels (notice how each one is different)

Enjoying animation

Today, watching animated films is a really popular pastime. A lot of cartoons are now made with the aid of computers. These do all the time-consuming drawing and painting. They can also produce complex, three-dimensional characters, or add cartoon elements to film of real actors.

FACT BOX

• A cine camera used for shooting cels is fixed so that it looks down on a flat baseboard. The cels for one frame are placed on the board and a photo is taken. Then the cels for the next frame are shot, and so on.

• Model animation is done with a rostrum camera, held firm so that it does not shift between frames. However, it can be tilted, panned (moved to follow a moving object) and zoomed.

• With model animation, there are around 25 frames for every second of finished film.

This little picture appears in the top right-hand corner of every other page. Flick all the pages of the book quickly and watch the pictures. What happens?

EASY ANIMATION

A 19th century phenakistoscope. Each image is slightly different. When you spin the disc, you see an action sequence through the slots.

Dᴜʀɪɴɢ the 19th century, there was a craze for optical toys, such as flick-books. Many of them created an illusion of movement by displaying a sequence of pictures in quick succession. At first, the pictures were hand-drawn. Later, photos taken by early cine cameras were used as well. Here, you can find out how to make a toy called a phenakistoscope, and how to use it to turn a series of pictures into an animation. Our toy is slightly different to the Victorian one on the left, as the slots on the one you will make are on the outside.

Make your own phenakistoscope

You will need: thick card, paper, ruler, sharp pencil, scissors, sticky tape, glue, dark felt-tip pen, camera, models.

1 On card, draw a disc about 25 cm across. Draw eight equal segments on it. At the end of each segment line, draw slots 4 cm long and ½ cm wide.

2 Now cut out your disc, and the slots around the outside of it. Make sure that the slots are no wider than ½ cm.

3 On pieces of light-coloured paper, draw a series of eight pictures. These should form a movement sequence. Make sure that your drawings are fairly simple and clear, and that they are drawn with a clean, strong line.

4 Fix the pictures to the disc, just under the slots. Push a pencil through the centre of the card.

5 Stand in front of a mirror. Hold the disc vertical, with the pictures towards the mirror. Spin the disc and look through the slots. You should see an animated loop of action in the mirror.

Photo phenakistoscope

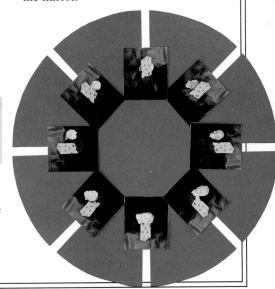

1 Now try a model animation. Take eight photographs of a model from the same position (use a tripod if you can). Move the model(s) slightly each time. The models should take up the middle third of the photograph frame.

2 Cut your photos to size and stick them to the phenakistoscope, one under each slot. Your phenakistoscope *(right)* will work better if the side next to your eye is a dark colour. Just cover it roughly with a black felt-tip pen.

CAMERAS IN SCIENCE

MOST of us use our cameras for recording holidays and special occasions, or for taking snaps of our friends. Photography is also extremely important in science and technology. For example, it is used for recording images that have been made by scientific instruments, so that they can be studied later. It is also used to record experiments that happen too fast for the human eye to see, and for analysing experimental results. In many modern scientific instruments, electronic cameras have taken the place of film cameras. Their images can be transferred easily to computer for analysis.

Some special microscopes (above) can take very detailed close-up photos. You can also do the same thing with a normal microscope, by fitting an SLR camera to it. You remove the SLR's lens and the microscope acts as a close-up lens for the camera.

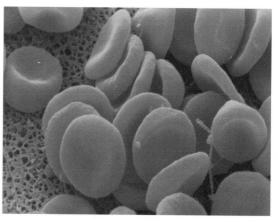

Microscope photographs
A photograph taken with a microscope is called a photomicrograph *(above)*. This photomicrograph is a close-up of cells in our blood called red blood cells.

Photographing heat
All objects give off heat rays called infra-red rays. Hotter objects give off stronger rays. A special type of film called infra-red film is sensitive to heat rays rather than light rays. Hot and cold objects show up in different colours or shades.

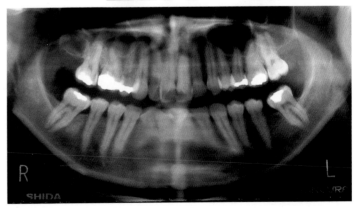

When you are taking photos of the sky with a telescope, using long exposures, the telescope often has to move slowly across the sky. This is to stop the stars from becoming streaks on your final pictures.

Photographing the stars

Just as a camera can be added to a microscope to take close-up pictures, one can also be added to a telescope. The telescope acts like a very powerful telephoto lens for the camera. (A telephoto lens makes distant objects seem much closer.) Light from the stars is very weak, and so long exposures are needed.

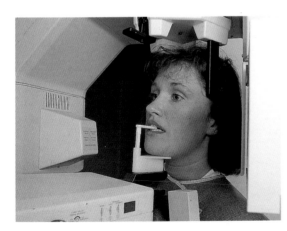

X-ray images

An X-ray picture is simply film that has been processed – a negative. X-rays help dentists *(above)* and doctors to find out all kinds of things about the body.

Where more X-rays reach the film, through soft parts of the body, the film turns a darker tone when it is developed. Bones and teeth (above) *show up white.*

CAMERAS AND COMPUTERS

PHOTOGRAPHS are often used in computer applications. For example, a multimedia CD-ROM about nature might contain thousands of photographs of animals and plants. Photographs stored and displayed by computer are called digital images because they consist of a long series of numbers rather than a real photograph on paper. They are either real photographs that have been put into a computer scanner to turn them into digital form, or they have been photographed with a digital, film-less, camera. Digital images can be copied over and over again, without any loss in quality. This means that they can be sent easily from one computer to another – over the Internet, for example.

Just like ordinary cameras, digital cameras come as compacts and SLRs. They have a lens and shutter, but, in the space where the film would normally be, they have a special light-sensitive microchip. This means that the photographs are stored in the camera's memory.

FACT BOX
• The highest resolution digital cameras divide a picture into a grid about 7000 pixels wide and 5000 pixels deep.

• Many digital pictures use 24-bit colour. This means that each pixel can be any one of 16,771,216 different colours.

Video phone
The digital video camera on top of this computer takes pictures that are sent down the telephone line and appear on another computer's screen. This lets the people at both computers see each other.

Pixel pictures

A digital image is made up of pixels, or dots. A number represents the colour of each tiny dot. High-resolution images divide the picture into a greater number of smaller dots than low-resolution ones, but they take up more computer memory.

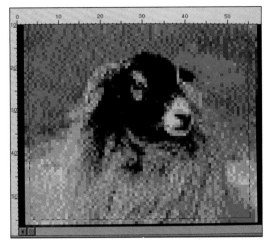

This shows a digitized picture on a computer screen, before it has been manipulated.

Here is the same picture after it has been manipulated by computer. Can you see how it has changed?

Retouching

Once a photo is digitized, it can be altered in any way by the computer. For example, colours can be changed or another photo can be added in. A polar bear could be put in a desert! It is much easier than trying the same thing with photography.

INDEX

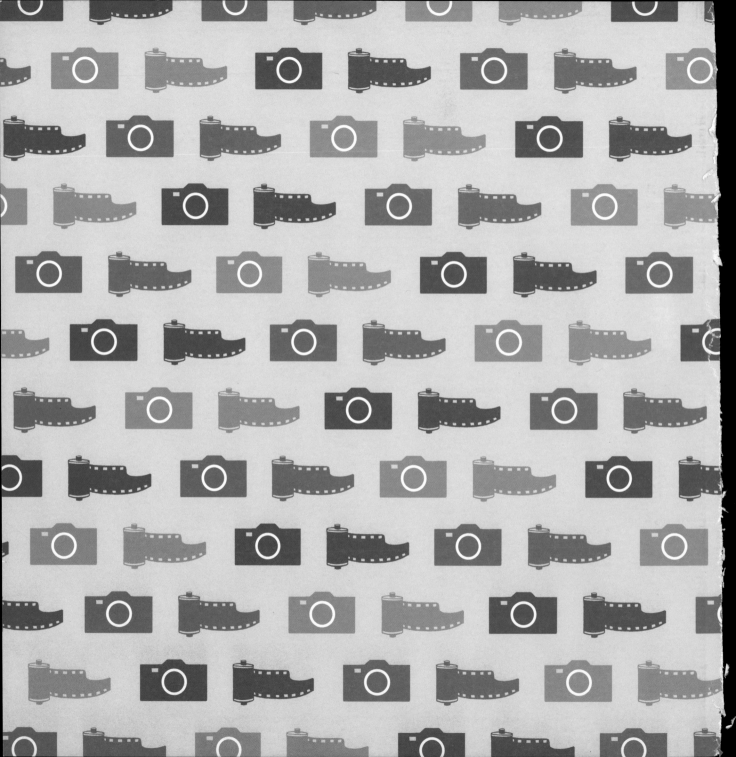